Mighty Machines

MONSTER TRUCKS

Ian Graham

QEB Publishing

Copyright © QEB Publishing, Inc. 2008

Published in the United States by
QEB Publishing, Inc.
3 Wrigley, Suite A
Irvine, CA 92618

www.qed-publishing.co.uk

Library of Congress Control Number: 2008010024

ISBN 978 1 60992 359 4

Printed in China

Author Ian Graham
Designers Phil and Traci Morash
Editor Paul Manning
Picture Researcher Claudia Tate

Picture credits (t = top, b = bottom, FC = front cover)
AFP/Getty Images Oliver Lang 16
Artemis Images Pikes Peak Hill Climb 10
Clive Featherby 9t
Corbis Richard T Nowitz 17, Transtock 18, Ross Pictures 21
Frankish Enterprises 14b
Getty Images Tim de Frisco 7t
Reuters/Corbis Regis Duvignau 5t, Rick Fowler 20
Rex Features Justin Downing 12, SIPA 6
Shutterstock Michael Stokes FC 8, Maksim Shmeljov 6, 11t, 13,
Barry Salmons 15, Khafizov Ivan Harisovich 18;
TS/Keystone USA/Rex Features 4

Words in **bold** can be found in the glossary on page 23.

Contents

What are monster trucks?

Monster trucks are the world's biggest, fastest, and most powerful trucks.

Monster trucks with extra-large wheels thrill the crowds at truck shows, while other giant trucks move the biggest and heaviest loads.

When a huge load has to be moved by road, only a giant truck can do the job.

Monster trucks often have tires as tall as a normal-sized car!

tire

Bigfoot
monster trucks

The world's first monster truck was Bigfoot 1. It was built in 1975 from an ordinary **pick-up truck**, but special wheels and parts were added to make it bigger and better.

After Bigfoot 1, lots more Bigfoot monster trucks were built.

The wheels of Bigfoot trucks are so huge that children can easily stand inside them!

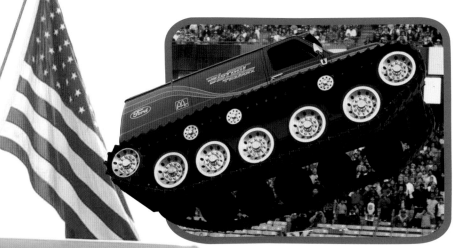

Bigfoot Fastrax is different from the other Bigfoots because it has tank tracks instead of wheels.

Car crushers

Car crushing is a favorite event in monster truck shows. The trucks drive over the top of scrap cars and squash them flat.

With their huge weight and powerful wheels, monster trucks make short work of flattening cars.

To make car crushing safe, car **batteries**, **fuel**, and glass must be removed first. Drivers must also wear fireproof suits and crash helmets.

How would YOU like a ride in this champion car crusher?

Monster racers

Races between monster trucks are held in **stadiums**, on race tracks, and on closed roads. In a hill climb, the trucks race up a dirt track to the top of a hill.

Not all racing trucks are giant-sized. Some are ordinary road trucks. Others are built specially for racing on **circuits**.

A powerful racing truck roars around a bend in a twisting hill-climb race.

Big crowds turn out
to watch their favorite
trucks compete in races
and other stadium events.

Truck **stunts** and **tricks**

In the **freestyle** part of a monster truck show, drivers make their trucks do amazing tricks and stunts.

The crowds love to see the trucks jump into the air, ride over ramps, do **wheelies,** and spin around on end!

The roof of a monster truck must be strong to protect the driver if the truck turns over.

A monster truck jumps into the air during a freestyle competition.

LUCAS OIL

Monster stars

The leading monster trucks are as famous as pop stars. Each one has a different name and is painted in its own special style.

Jurassic Attack is painted to look like a dinosaur's head.

Fans of the trucks cheer them on as they battle it out in competitions and races.

Samson's bulging muscles look as if they mean business!

Road giants

While monster trucks and car crushers entertain the crowds, hardworking giant trucks **haul** some of the biggest, heaviest, and longest loads ever carried on wheels.

The part of the truck that does the pulling is called the tractor. Behind it, the trailer carries the load.

Imagine seeing a whole house coming toward you along the road!

This huge trailer is carrying parts of an Airbus A380—the biggest aircraft ever built!

tractor

trailer

Monster miners

The biggest trucks in the world are called dump trucks. Their job is to haul huge loads of rock dug from under the ground. The rock often contains valuable metals, such as copper.

These trucks can never leave the **mines** where they work, because they are far too big to go on ordinary roads.

The biggest dump trucks are so huge that the driver has to climb a set of steps to reach the **cab**.

Giant dump trucks need even bigger machines to load them.

NASA's giants

The space agency NASA has two giant vehicles to transport its huge space shuttle craft to the **launch pad**. These two monsters are called crawler-transporters.

tracks

Each crawler-transporter runs on eight **tracks** powered by electric motors.

space shuttle

The crawler-transporters were first built in the 1960s. At that time they were the biggest tracked vehicles ever made.

Because of their size, crawler-transporters can only move at a snail's pace. This huge vehicle weighs 2,870 tons (2,603 tonnes) and carries around 5,000 gallons (19,000 liters) of fuel.

United States

Behind You, Discovery!

Activities

- Which of these trucks is doing a wheelie?

- Make a drawing of your own monster truck with extra-big wheels. Think of a name for it and then color it to suit its name.

- Look at these pictures. Which one is a dump truck?

- Can you remember what NASA's giant crawler-transporters carry?

Glossary

Battery
The part that supplies electricity to a car or truck.

Cab
The part of a truck where the driver sits.

Circuit
A track built specially for racing.

Crawler-transporter
A vehicle that runs on tracks for moving very large or heavy loads.

Freestyle
Part of a monster truck show where drivers do tricks and stunts.

Fuel
Liquid burned in a truck's engine to provide power to turn the wheels.

Haul
To transport or carry by truck.

Launch pad
The platform from which a rocket takes off.

Mine
A place where coal and rocks are dug out of the ground.

Pick-up truck
A light truck with low sides.

Stadium
A sports ground with seats where people watch races and other events.

Tracks
Metal belts around a heavy vehicle's wheels to spread the weight.

Wheelies
When a truck stands up or drives along on just its back wheels.

Index